ISBN 978-1-332-94956-4
PIBN 10441870

1 MONTH OF
FREE
READING

at

www.ForgottenBooks.com

By purchasing this book you are eligible for one month membership to ForgottenBooks.com, giving you unlimited access to our entire collection of over 1,000,000 titles via our web site and mobile apps.

To claim your free month visit:

www.forgottenbooks.com/free441870

English
Français
Deutsche
Italiano
Español
Português

www.forgottenbooks.com

Mythology Photography **Fiction**
Fishing Christianity **Art** Cooking
Essays Buddhism Freemasonry
Medicine **Biology** Music **Ancient
Egypt** Evolution Carpentry Physics
Dance Geology **Mathematics** Fitness
Shakespeare **Folklore** Yoga Marketing
Confidence Immortality Biographies
Poetry **Psychology** Witchcraft
Electronics Chemistry History **Law**
Accounting **Philosophy** Anthropology
Alchemy Drama Quantum Mechanics
Atheism Sexual Health **Ancient History**
Entrepreneurship Languages Sport
Paleontology Needlework Islam
Metaphysics Investment Archaeology
Parenting Statistics Criminology
Motivational

The LARK Edition

THE MAN WITH THE HOE

MARKHAM

Date Due

The Lark Editions

A SELECTION of modern classics, with illustrations by modern artists; in dainty form; paper boards, 75c., and *éditions de luxe*.

I. •KIPLING.   *Mandalay.*   Illustrated by Robert Edgren.

II. MARKHAM.   *The Man with the Hoe.*   Illustrated by Porter Garnett.

In preparation

III. KIPLING.   *Recessional.*   Illustrated by Florence Lundborg.

IV. KIPLING.   *The Vampire.*   Illustrated by Lander Phelps.

To be followed by others.

The Lark Edition

The Man with

the Hoe

Edwin Markham

The
Man with the
Hoe

Edwin
Markham

With Illustrations
by Porter Garnett

Doxey's
At the Sign of The Lark
New York

The
Man with the
Hoe

Edwin
Markham

With illustrations
by Porter Garnett

Doxey's

At the Sign of The Lark

New York

UNIVERSITY PRESS · JOHN WILSON
AND SON · CAMBRIDGE, U.S.A.

*Reprinted as originally published
in the "San Francisco Examiner"*

The illustrations and decorative designs
in this volume are by Porter Garnett

The Man with the Hoe

The MAN WITH THE HOE

God made Man in His own Image, in the Image of God made He him.

 owed by the weight
of centuries he leans
Upon his hoe and
gazes on the ground,
he emptiness of ages in his
face,
nd on his back the burden
of the world.

The Man with the Hoe

ho loosened and let down
  this brutal jaw?
hose was the hand that
  slanted back this brow?
hose breath blew out the
  light within this brain?

ho made him dead to rap-
ture and despair,
thing that grieves not and
that never hopes,
tolid and stunned, a brother
to the ox?

The Man with the Hoe

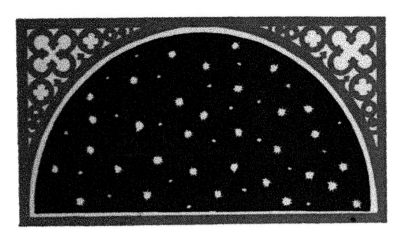

s this the Thing the Lord
God made and gave

o have dominion over sea
and land;

o trace the stars and search
the heavens for power;

o feel the passion of Eter-
nity?

The Man with the Hoe

s this the Dream He dreamed
who shaped the suns
nd pillared the blue firma-
ment with light?

The Man with the Hoe

own all the stretch of hell
   to its last gulf
here is no shape more terri-
   ble than this—
ore tongued with censure of
   the world's blind greed—
ore filled with signs and por-
   tents for the soul—
ore fraught with menace to
   the universe.

The Man with the Hoe

hat gulfs between him and
the seraphim !

lave of the wheel of labor,
what to him

re Plato and the swing of
Pleiades?

hat the long reaches of the
peaks of song,

he rift of dawn, the redden-
ing of the rose?

hrough this dread shape the
suffering ages look;
ime's tragedy is in that
aching stoop;
brough this dread shape
humanity betrayed,
lundered, profaned and dis-
inherited,
ries protest to the Judges of
the World,
protest that is also proph-
ecy.

The Man with the Hoe

masters, lords and rulers in
all lands,
s this the handiwork you
give to God,
his monstrous thing distorted
and soul-quenched?

The Man with the Hoe

ow will you ever straighten
up this shape;

ive back the upward looking
and the light;

ebuild in it the music and
the dream;

ouch it again with immor-
tality;

ake right the immemorial
infamies,

erfidious wrongs, immedica-
ble woes?

The Man with the Hoe

masters, lords and rulers in
all lands,

ow will the Future reckon
with this Man?

ow answer his brute question
in that hour

hen whirlwinds of rebellion
shake the world?

The Man with the Hoe

ow will it be with kingdoms
and with kings —
ith those who shaped him to
the thing he is —
hen this dumb Terror shall
reply to God,
fter the silence of the centuries?